D0832514

50
LOW COST
WAYS
TO ACQUIRE
NEW CUSTOMERS

ACTion Press
Phoenix, Arizona

Increased Profits Through Knowledge™

Request for permissions should be addressed to: The ACT Group, Inc., 201 West Orchid Lane, Phoenix, Arizona 85021. (800) 515-0034.
www.NoPressureSelling.com

Library of Congress Catalog Card Number: 89-86059

International Standard Book Number 0-9624624-0-3

Printed in the United States of America.

Twelfth Printing 2008

For Charlotte,
my wife and best friend

Table of Contents

Foreword

"It is tragic that in today's great competitive market, very few people realize that one can have the finest products and services, and yet remain the best kept secret in our economic system.

Those companies and individuals that soar to the top are those that follow the principles so clearly and powerfully set forth in this book.

Steve Howard, through years of study and successful experience, has mastered a "HOW-TO" program that is invaluable to those who are not willing to follow a path of mediocrity.

50 Low Cost Ways To Acquire New Customers, not only shows how to follow the basic principles that lead to corporate and individual greatness, but also explains in detail many neglected opportunities such as barter, negotiations, cable TV, news releases, networking and many others.

I join others in saying without reservation that this book is one of the finest and most valuable of its kind available today."

> *Cavett Robert*
> *Founder*
> *National Speakers Association*

Introduction

One secret to your company's future growth and prosperity is the ability to attract new customers. The more methods you can successfully employ to tell people about your company and why they should do business with you, the more new customers you will acquire.

Many businesses with limited advertising budgets spend their money on the wrong advertising, promotion and lead generation programs only to obtain poor results and frustrations for their efforts. This book outlines 50 common sense ways you can acquire new customers at little or no expense. These ideas are easy to implement and modify to fit your situation. Because of their low cost and flexibility, they are ideal marketing tools for this era of rapid change. If you think one of the methods will work for you and it doesn't, you will not have wasted a fortune trying it. Once you determine which ideas work best for your company, repeat and fine-tune them for maximum results. As you study the ideas, ask yourself how you can use or modify each one to match your business needs and deliver new customers, both now and in the future.

1. Plan for Success

The old maxim, "If you fail to plan, you have planned to fail," is true. To begin your plan, grab your calendar and schedule two to four hours for a planning session away from the distractions of your daily routine. All you need are open minds, a flip chart, and the outlines on pages 86, 87, 88 and 89. If you have a medium-size company, each front line manager should meet with his or her team members. All of the employees of a very small firm should be able to meet as one group.

Each employee plays a critical role in the success of your plan to bring in new customers. When employees are included in the planning process, an interesting

1

event occurs: They get personally involved and become "owners" of the ideas the plan contains. Ownership of ideas is one of the great secrets of motivation. History has shown time and again that people are much more willing to work for their ideas and beliefs, than those of others. Motivated people not only help bring in new customers, they will do whatever is necessary to keep them coming back.

Following the information gathering session, use the data you have collected to develop your plan.

1. **Plan on paper.** The only plan is a written plan because it adds discipline and helps propel good intentions into action. Rewrite the information from the flip chart onto 8½"x 11" paper and insert the pages into a three-ring binder. Add a summary page at the front and check it at least once per week to see if you are staying on target. The 12-Month Plan on pages 90 and 91 will be helpful in accomplishing your goals.

2. **Keep your plan simple.** You want it to be a usable living blueprint, not a document that sits in your bookcase collecting dust.

3. **Set specific goals.** Assign personal responsibilities (e.g., who is to do what and when).

4. **Prioritize potential customers.** Eighty percent of your new business will come from 20 percent of your target customers. To help you locate your best new customers seek clients who are similar to your most profitable current ones.

5. **Establish a budget.** Determine how much money you can afford to allot for advertising, lead generation and promotion (use a percentage of your projected gross sales for the next 12 months). Allocate funds based on the greatest benefits at the lowest cost.

6. **Plan for promotions.** The next 12 months should be blocked off in promotion periods (e.g., "tour of our facilities," "spring and fall seminar," and "quarterly direct mailing programs").

7. **Plan for problems.** Things always take longer and cost more than predicted. Keep asking "What if?" Look for problems you can correct before they happen.

8. **Plan for profitability.** Focus on low-cost advertising and lead generation to bring in new customers, not lowering your prices and profit margins. Demand increases profitability; determine how you can create demand by providing something unique, adding extra value or education of future customers.

9. **Plan your message.** Remember, people don't buy products and services, they buy the benefits, results and solutions they offer.

10. **Anticipate change and follow-up.** Since change is the only constant, plan ahead and prepare any data necessary to change your strategy with conditions. Follow up and determine how you will be there when your future customers' needs change.

2. *Know Your Customers*

One of the most overlooked methods of acquiring new customers is to gain an understanding of current customers. When they make a purchase from you, what are they really buying? If you own a clothing store, are they buying protection from the elements, or style, image, and prestige? If you don't know your customers you will waste your time and money offering the wrong benefits to the wrong people. Remember, people don't buy your product or service for what it is, they buy it for what it does specifically for them.

The best way to become acquainted with your customers is to ask them the right questions. Why do they buy from your firm? How did they hear about you? What benefits do they want most?

Know your customers' ZIP codes and use them to gain valuable information about them and their neighbors (your future customers). Most libraries have a copy of *The Sourcebook of Demographics and Buying Power for Every ZIP Code in the USA*. This powerful publication details (by zip code): population; annual projected growth; number of households; housing profile by percentage owned and rented; age of homes; median value of homes; age distribution and median age of those living in each area; median household income; distribution of households by income, education, employment profile, and average travel time to work; purchasing potential index for several areas, including loans, groceries, and auto aftermarket; and much more.

Another good way to become acquainted with your customers' industry is to enroll in college or junior college courses pertaining to that industry. If you don't have time to attend those classes, most college bookstores have texts covering various businesses and industries. Perhaps you can attend your customers' seminars and training programs. Ask one of your key customers to inform you when the next one is scheduled.

When dealing with specific businesses and industries, learn your customers' language. People in most industries speak in shortcut language called jargon. Using your customers' jargon in marketing messages and face-to-face meetings can give you a distinct advantage over any competition. By knowing your customers, you don't have to waste time learning their business and problems, you can focus 100 percent of your attention on solving their problems.

3. Know Your Competition

Many successful businesses realize that the more they understand their competitors, the easier it is to acquire their customers. Let's face it, your competition wants your customers and you want theirs. Due to specialization, you may have only four or five major competitors in your area. Consider starting a file on each one. It should contain their print and Yellow Pages ads, brochures, coupons, etc.

Know your competitors' strengths and weaknesses. Understand everything your firm can provide your future customers that your competition cannot. Determine needs that your current and future customers have which have been overlooked by competitors. Think about how your firm can customize an existing product or service, or even add a new one that could help you develop new customers.

Your competition not only includes businesses similar to yours, it is anything that competes for your prospects' money. A luxury auto dealer's competition could include a fine jewelry store, a cruise ship line, or a cabin for sale in the woods. Winning in business, as in sports, requires acquiring as much knowledge as possible about your opponents.

4. Avoid Your Competition's Mistakes

You should know as much about your competition as you do about your target customers. If you avoid the common mistakes your competitors make, the customers they lose can become yours. Seven of the most common mistakes many businesses make are:

1. **Not following up.** When you are persistent and follow up, you may be the only one there when your future customers' needs change.

5

2. **Bad-mouthing the competition.** Slamming the competition gives them an advantage. If a potential customer asks about your competitor, use a simple statement like "They're good, but I believe our service is better because . . ."
3. **Assuming the sale ended when the product was sold.** A tremendous amount of future sales and referrals are lost simply because no one stayed in touch after a customer made a purchase.
4. **Bidding instead of selling.** Many firms assume that having the lowest price is the only thing that matters, but nothing could be further from the truth. The selling price will always be too high until value is established by explaining all of the ways your future customer will benefit from your solution to his problems.
5. **Taking advantage of current customers** by charging them a little extra to cover discounts and specials only new customers receive.
6. **Neglecting customers** or treating them with indifference. Seven out of ten customers who switch to a competitor cite poor service as the number one reason.
7. **Waiting for the phone to ring.** Anyone who thinks he can acquire profitable new business year after year by waiting for the phone to ring is only kidding himself. You have to constantly tell people why they should be doing business with you.

5. *Enlist Your Employees*

Each employee should understand that bringing in new customers is vital to the success of your business. When they are motivated, it's easy for them to keep their eyes on the goal. Whenever an employee secures a new customer, let him know how much you appreciate it.

6

Routinely recognize those employees who help bring in new customers or do something noteworthy to keep a current customer satisfied and loyal. *Behavior that is reinforced is repeated.*

There is one simple way all of your employees can bring in new customers. Provide each with business cards imprinted with their name. Business cards also give your employees a sense of belonging and being an important part of the company family.

Encourage your employees to give a card to everyone they meet. Two cards should be given to anyone who might know someone who could become your customer. Human nature being what it is, people will throw away an expensive four-color brochure, but they will keep a business card.

- The business cards should be attractive.
- They should project your company's image.
- Consider a quality stock, raised letters and two or more colors.
- An up-to-date logo adds to a card's impact.
- Use the standard 3½" x 2" card size. Odd shapes or oversized cards will not fit into your future customer's business card file system.
- Include home telephone numbers under the business number for a powerful effect.
- On the back of each card, consider listing all of your products and services, or the benefits of dealing with your firm.

Business cards can be a high-quality, low-cost "mini-brochure" which projects your firm's professional image.

There are many way to keep your employees motivated and introducing new customers. Employee motivation is only one of the many benefits a routine training program can provide.

7

People Are
Six Times More
Likely to Rely On
the Judgement of Others
Than on Advertising
When Making a
Buying Decision

6. *Train Your Employees*

A lead is *not* a sale. At best, it is only an opportunity to make a sale. Selling is a skill that must be learned. Some form of sales and marketing training — including methods to turn leads into sales, informing others about your company and offering the benefits of your firm's products and services, must be part of every one of your employees' job description.

Customer service training is vital. Everyone in an organization needs it. Even the most conscientious employee can be offensive and not realize it. If a potential customer's impression of your organization is poor, chances are that all of the time and money you have invested in advertising and lead generation will be wasted. Until someone demonstrates a better way, people will continue making the same costly mistakes.

Training is the only vehicle that can provide the new skills and knowledge necessary to enable profitable change. Some things to keep in mind when training employees include:

• Schedule routine training sessions, even during the busiest time of the year.
• Consider a weekly 30-minute to one-hour training program before work.
• A few minutes of open discussion may be invaluable.
• Training information to be included depends upon your firm's needs and each employee's level of experience.
• Find an employee or manager willing to take total responsibility for training.
• Consider asking each employee to present a different topic at each meeting.
• Focus on one concept per training session.
• Provide a training guide and encourage note-taking.

- Encourage discussion and answer questions immediately.
- Positive suggestions and ideas that develop should be immediately acted upon.
- If it's technical it's changing. If you provide a technical product or service make sure those delivering it have the latest information.
- Consider using manufacturers' and distributors' training programs and instructors.
- For added impact, introduce a professional sales trainer once or twice per year.

When your staff is properly trained, motivated, and included in your plan to get new customers, growth and prosperity is no longer a goal, it's a reality.

7. Request Referrals

Studies show that people are six times more likely to rely on the judgment of others than on advertising when making a buying decision. Up to 80 percent of all consumer choices are the result of personal recommendations. Satisfied customers are a leading source of new customers. Referrals work because people prefer buying what has been accepted by others. People value certainty over uncertainty, and the opinions of others minimize risk. Referrals give your firm the instant credibility that other forms of lead generation can't provide.

There are two requirements for getting referrals: You must be worthy of them and you must request them. The more you exceed your customers' expectations, the more referrals you'll receive. Satisfied customers will gladly inform others about your good products and superior service.

After establishing a relationship built on trust, ask your customers for the names of three or four people who they know that you can help. *Be specific.* Help your customers think about the people they know at their clubs, in their office buildings or in positions similar to theirs. Consider asking your customers if they would call the referral for you. They can say good things about you that you can't say or advertise.

After a purchase has been made, consider sending a short "customer satisfaction survey" to each customer. At the bottom you can request referrals. "If your are happy with our product/service you can reward us by giving us referrals."

Always follow up on referrals as soon as possible. Take the time to acknowledge anyone who refers a new customer. At the very minimum send a thank you note. If warranted, send a small gift, it can help assure a steady supply of new referral customers.

Involve your entire organization. Place a "Think Referrals" poster in a conspicuous location. Getting referrals from every customer should be your team's number one marketing priority.

8. Get Placed on Referral Lists

Many consumers contact a product's manufacturer when they encounter a problem or need service. Some manufacturers and distributors have a consumers' hot line or referral network. The key to getting leads from manufacturers and distributors, is to request them — several times if necessary.

Leads from a manufacturer provide instant credibility. Your future customers believe that you must know what you're doing, or the manufacturer would not have referred you.

11

Many trade associations provide referrals on a rotating basis to their members in good standing. Obtaining referrals from your trade association also provides credibility, especially if the association has a code of ethics to which its members must adhere.

As with all referrals, show your appreciation to the manufacturers, distributors or trade associations who provide them. You may be pleasantly surprised how many more referrals you will subsequently receive.

9. *Network*

Networking allows you to contact many important people who you don't have the time or money to reach otherwise. It works because most people enjoy helping those they know. We all feel good when we can direct someone to a product or service that will help them. Just one network contact can open the door to many new customers.

Think about all of the places you go: church, a favorite restaurant, health club, association meetings, etc. Network by:

- Getting to know as many people as possible.
- Attending your customer's meetings.
- Making yourself visible.
- Being helpful and friendly.
- Being enthusiastic.
- Freely sharing your knowledge.
- Letting people know why they and others they know need you and your firm's products and services.
- Exchange business cards and note on the back additional important information.
- Keep your network contact's business cards in a filing system and regularly review it.

Leads groups are another form of networking. They meet in nearly every city in the United States. Some formal leads groups have well over 100 members. Usually only one person is allowed to join from each type of business or industry. For example, there can be only one accountant, one clothing store owner, one office supplier, etc. At each meeting, one member explains something about his business that will be of value to all of the group's members. Someone may discuss new businesses moving into the area and "lead cards" are exchanged.

One type of less formal leads group consists of a handful of business or salespeople who call on or have the same type of customers but do not have a competing product or service. A weekly breakfast meeting can provide an ideal opportunity to share information about the customers they call upon. Each person brings three leads that include the contact person's name, address, phone number and the best way and time to contact the decision makers.

Other valuable information about potential customers is also exchanged (e.g., she won't accept gifts, or he enjoys discussing business while playing golf). Information concerning expansion plans or merger possibilities is also discussed.

The best way to locate a leads group is to ask your suppliers, business people who are close to you, or members of your club or civic organization. If you can't find a leads group, start one. Regularly meeting with four or five positive people who share your problems, frustrations and accomplishments will not only help you find new customers but will also keep your attitude charged up. Remember, wherever there are people, there is an opportunity to network.

10. Become a Member

Given a choice, we would all rather do business with friends. Membership in clubs, associations and religious groups provides us with an opportunity to contribute something positive while building friendships which can lead to new customers. Membership in your industry's trade associations shows stability and credibility while demonstrating to your future customers that you're in business for the long haul.

Consider joining your customer's trade associations. The key to locating new customers is becoming involved. Take a position on a committee then gain a leadership role and become well-acquaintedwith the other members. Attend seminars that your customers' trade associations sponsor, even if they are not in your field of expertise. You'll gain a better understanding of your customers' problems and opportunities will arise to familiarize yourself with some of the more influential members.

The best way to turn members into customers is by presenting training programs and seminars in your area of specialization. Not only will you be viewed as an expert, you can position yourself as a problem-solver. Whenever a member has a need for products or services your firm offers, they'll think of you first.

11. Use Direct Mail

Direct mail is a leading method used to communicate your message to prospective customers. Direct mail sends your marketing message to "targeted" customers. The exciting aspect of direct mail is the ability to zero in on just those folks you want as new customers.

**The Exciting Aspect
of Direct Mail
is the Ability
to Zero in on
Just Those Folks
You Want as New Customers**

Your direct mail mailing list is of major importance to your program. Use several simple methods to acquire mailing lists of your future customers. Start by looking in the Yellow Pages under "Mailing Lists." The trade and civic organizations that your prospects attend also may have mailing lists and preprinted labels available for $40 to $80 per 1,000 names. Additionally, publications that your target customers read usually sell mailing lists. One way to develop your own mailing list is to purchase a reverse directory from your phone company. (A reverse directory lists (in order) street address followed by name and phone number.) Using the reverse directory allows you to mail your message to those located adjacent to your finest current customers.

When designing your direct mail program, keep several things in mind:

- Expect a 1 percent response (although it may be higher). If a low response rate is unacceptable, direct mail may not be for you.
- Determine how your mailing piece will grab and hold a reader's attention (you have approximately 2 to 5 seconds to accomplish this task or it gets tossed).
- Always list your offering's benefits. (Remember, people don't buy the product/service, they buy what it does for them.)
- Use an attention-grabbing headline. (If the headline isn't strong, it will not be read.)
- Institute a call to action. (Motivate people to do what you want: pick up the phone and call for service, go to your store, put a check in the mail, or send in a postage-paid response card.)
- Keep in touch with your current customers with direct mail. Develop a mailing list for each customer and keep it up-to-date.

Your direct mail program must be well-planned. Start your program at least three months before you want your offer to reach prospective customers. It always takes more time than you expect to develop a brochure, circular or postcard; have it typeset and proofed; printed; labeled; stamped and mailed.

Direct mail, like other advertising, relies heavily on how many times your target customers receive your message. The more your message is seen, the higher its response rate will be. Consider two to four mailings per year to your best prospects. Keep your name visible. Track your results.

Start researching your program by saving some of the direct mail you receive at your home and office. Keep the best examples — the ones that tend to call you into action. Ask the members of your leads group which they prefer and why?

Because even one small change in copy or design can drastically affect the outcome of your direct mail program, it may be cost-effective to hire a professional copywriter and graphics designer to help get things started. Some of the companies who sell mailing lists can handle your entire direct mail program.

If you have a college or university in your area, consider hiring a senior marketing student to help design your direct mail program. This person may know other students who can design your direct mail piece and write effective copy. Most students enjoy working on a project like this because they can use the finished product to help them secure a job after graduation.

Test the results of your direct mail program. Try different headlines, artwork and copy. Make any necessary corrections and discover what works best before you mail to thousands of prospects. Remember, direct mail becomes junk mail only when it doesn't hit its target.

12. *Pinpoint New Customers*

Door hangers are a valuable tool to use in pinpointing your message to select target customers. Door hangers, or similar advertising devices can be delivered to only those houses you select (e.g., houses with slate roofs or Bermuda grass lawns, or homes that need new paint or have fireplaces).

Door hangers also can be used by a firm doing work in a particular location. For instance, a carpet company's installation team places door hangers on 20 houses near the home where they have recently installed new carpeting. Prior to the installation, the firm's receptionist secures the home owner's permission to use her name and address on 20 door hangers. The door hanger may read, "Mrs. Jones at 123 North St. is enjoying new carpeting from XYZ Carpet Company located at . . ."

Door hangers and other pinpoint marketing tools are effective for several reasons: First, cost is low. Secondly, usually houses on the same street are the same age. Thus, it stands to reason that if Mrs. Jones needed new carpeting, several of her neighbors probably do, too. Thirdly, you can include a special limited time offer or coupon to promote quick response.

Door hangers can be delivered for less than the cost of postage. Consider contacting the Boy Scout or Girl Scout council in your area for the telephone number of the troop nearest you. Other groups that may deliver pinpoint messages are ball teams, school clubs and church youth groups.

13. *Develop a Brochure*

A brochure's purpose is to provide overall information about your company or the products/services you offer. In addition, you can include specific details and answers to questions your prospects will likely ask.

Besides serving as a great direct mail piece, brochures can be used at trade shows, with sales letters, distributed by members of your leads group and employed during face-to-face sales calls. Brochures are ideal as a follow-up sales tool when a prospect requests more information from the tag line in your print ad: "Call for our free brochure today." Data show that over 25 percent of those requesting a brochure will ultimately make a purchase.

Brochures don't have to be expensive to be effective. Some tips to help you develop a simple brochure include:

- Consider one that uses standard paper sizes (8½" x 11" or 8½" x 14").
- Use at least two colors. The second color should be used for headlines and to highlight main points.
- Use bold print or italics to capture your readers' attention.
- Consider using black and white photos of your employees in action.
- Brochure copy can be written by someone in your firm, or perhaps by a student or freelance writer. A professional writer's fee may range from $20 to $60 per hour.
- Write about the benefits your firm offers your customers. Explain how your firm is unique. Relate the services you provide that your competition doesn't.
- List your firm's phone number in more than one place.
- If you don't have a printer, obtain at least two estimates and study recent samples of their work before investing your marketing dollars.

Estimated printing costs for 2,500 high-quality, entry level brochures could include the following:

Typesetting $100
70# coated stock 425
Folding 25
2 black and white photos (halftones) 20

Total $570

The manufacturer of the products you sell may have several brochures you can obtain at little or no cost. In many cases, all you have to do is print your name, address and phone number on them to "make them yours".

14. Use Discount Coupons

Over 160 billion coupons are distributed every year. Over 71 percent of the nation's household shoppers use coupons. When there are four or more persons in the household, the number jumps to 87 percent using coupons. Look around your home or office, chances are you have one or more of these "mini-ads" stuck to your refrigerator, in your car or in your purse or wallet waiting to be used.

Coupons can cause consumers to change to a different supplier for their product or service. According to research, if a coupon was issued for a product found to be unavailable in the store where a person usually shops, 25 percent would travel to another store looking for the offer, 32 percent would completely postpone the purchase, 23 percent would purchase a different brand and only 12 percent would discard the coupon.

To work most efficiently, the discount must be worthwhile. On small ticket items a markdown of 20 percent should be a starting point. On larger items a fixed dollar amount (e.g., $5 off) usually works best.

Besides the offer, your coupon should include a time limit, your firm's name, address and phone number. Target your prospects, not current customers. If you are not careful, many of your already loyal customers may redeem your coupons.

Discount coupons can be placed in your circulars, printed in newspapers and magazines, sent directly to your target customer, or distributed in hundreds of other ways. The redemption rate of direct mail coupons is approximately 9 percent. Coupons included in newspaper inserts are redeemed at the rate of approximately 5 percent. The redemption decreases as the cost of the product or service increases. Study the discount coupons that come to you and borrow the best ideas.

Many businesses don't employ discount coupons because they fear they will lose money by attracting new customers who will purchase their product only one time. When used properly, nothing could be further from the truth. Over time and with good service, a new customer may buy hundreds of times the purchase price of the couponed product or service. In other words, discount coupons can spur a new customer to buy the product/service at least once and exceeding your new customers' expectations will keep them coming back for more.

15. *Put a Quick Printer on Your Team*

Your local quick printer can serve as an unrecognized source of marketing information for your area. Because those printers have been developing low-cost marketing tools for years, they usually have good ideas about what works and what doesn't. Many quick printers will gladly show you their past work. If you find an idea you like, why not alter it a bit to make it yours.

21

Some tools your quick printer has available include brochures, circulars, postcards and posters. Circulars provide less information than a brochure, but are less expensive and more flexible. They usually describe a special offer or announce a new service and can easily be designed with desktop publishing or typeset.

Usually circulars are printed on a standard-size page and can be cut to fit any size you want. A well-designed circular should arouse your target customer's desire to obtain your offer. Circulars can be distributed on street corners, in front of your store, door-to-door, at trade shows, placed under windshield wipers, pinned to bulletin boards, stuffed into bags and used as newspaper inserts. Because of their flexibility, they can also be used effectively in your direct mail program.

Postcards are the least expensive way to stay in touch with your current and future customers. They can be sent first class for less than a letter sent by bulk mail. This not only saves you money, but you can keep your mailing list current because undelivered first class mail is returned to the sender.

Since space is limited on a postcard, your message should be concise and well-thought-out. Consider reprinting one of your best print ads on the back of the postcard and place your "call to action" message on the front. Remember to leave enough space for your targeted customer's address.

Posters may be nothing more than an oversized circular on a heavy card stock. Your print ad artwork can be enlarged to create the poster's copy. Posters can be placed on telephone poles, in store windows and on bulletin boards.

Your quick printer has other low-cost marketing tools available. Plan on spending an hour with your quick printer and ask him or her to explain the services they can provide to help you reach new customers.

16. Write Sales Letters

You may be able to reach many future customers through sales letters. Even extremely busy people usually read a short letter that appears to be written directly to them.

Understand the needs of the person receiving your letter. Needs are discovered through fact finding. The better you know your prospective customers, the more effective your sales letter can be. For example, if you know your prospect's budget cycle, you can ensure your letter arrives at the appropriate time with the "right" message.

- Your sales letter is a reflection of your company's image.
- Your logo and letterhead should be professional and up-to-date.
- Your stationery and envelope should be of the highest quality.
- The letters should use accepted form and format.
- Your letter should maintain a personalized appearance, even though you will probably be using a word processor or electronic typewriter.
- Always send sales letters first class.
- Never use computer-printed labels.
- Have a call to action. Tell the reader what you want him or her to do, or explain what you will do (e.g., "For your convenience, I'll call your secretary on Monday the 18th to set up an appointment." Or "I'm free the after-

noon of the 20th or the morning of the 22nd, if either of these two days work for you.")
• Persistence pays. If your prospect is important enough for a sales letter, he or she is worth a follow-up phone call.
• Call 5 to 7 days after the letter was sent.
• Consider sending a different letter every month until you obtain the desired action. Include a pertinent magazine article or something of interest to high-priority prospects.

If you don't have a secretary or word processor, consider giving your mailing list of top prospects and a draft of your sales letter to a secretarial service. Sales letters work. Over time, your cost per new customer can remain quite low with this proven method of generating new customers.

17. Call Your Best Prospects

Prospecting for new customers is comparable to searching for gold. Calling your best prospects can be like mining the highest grade ore deposits. Costs of telephone sales calls are less than one-tenth that of a face-to-face sales call. Telephone calls allow you to establish a higher degree of rapport than letters or advertising.

When contacting "high quality" future customers by phone, there are several things to keep in mind:
• Persistence pays. Less than 10 out of 30 business calls are successfully connected on the first try.
• Know to whom you want to speak.
• Know as much as possible about the person and their firm. Determine the information you'll need to qualify the prospect and learn if there is an opportunity to help.

A Lead is Not a Sale
At Best
It Is Only
an Opportunity
to Make a Sale

- Use a well-planned opening statement. (Have a prepared script in front of you, but don't use it.)
- If possible, mention that you were referred by someone the prospect knows and respects.
- Within 30 seconds, explain why the person should listen to you.
- Explain how you will solve a problem or make their lives better.
- Show you understand the problems this person faces.
- Mirror the person's speech patterns. Speed up, slow down or pause.
- Reach your goal. Ask for either a face-to-face meeting or ask for the order.
- If you can't set up an immediate appointment, arrange for a future meeting.
- Be persistent, don't give up on your best prospects. In the movie "Wallstreet," Bud Fox called Gorden Geco 59 times before he finally got a face-to-face meeting.

18. Write Magazine and Newsletter Articles

One successful way to gain your target customers' attention is to routinely write articles for the publications they read. First you must collect and read many of the publications that your target customers read. (Your current customers may have past issues they will give or lend to you and subscription information is contained in the masthead.) Attempt to determine the most pressing needs of this group. Even if you don't write a word, this information will be invaluable.

Next, contact the publication's editor. Ask if the magazine would consider your submission of an article on a specific topic, which you have identified as timely and important. Tell the editor that you will submit the article as a service to the magazine's readers and there will be no charge. After you secure acceptance of your proposal, ask if there is any information you need to know about. Most magazines will gladly send you their writer's guidelines. These are invaluable as they detail manuscript specifications (e.g., length of manuscript, use of photographs, style guide of magazine, and magazine's article preferences). In addition, the editor may inform you of upcoming edition themes.

Choose a short, snappy title but remember that it probably will be changed. Start writing by using short paragraphs and familiar words. Copy should be double-spaced and neatly typed. Write your article with the purpose of duplicating it after it is published so you can send a copy to prospective customers. If practical, ask someone in your organization or a freelance editor to check the copy before it is submitted.

Once your articles are well-received, ask to write a monthly column. Send a 5" x 7" black and white photograph of yourself so it can be included in each issue. Ask your editor to include a tag line at the end of each article that lists your firm's name, address and phone number. This encourages readers (prospects) to contact you with questions they may have.

19. Write News Releases

The purpose of a news release is to get free publicity. It is the vehicle to use when approaching the media with information about your firm.

Because most people trust news more than advertising, a news release can provide a better chance of winning new customers than the most expensive advertising campaign. After a news release appears, use it in your marketing. Make reprints of it and use them in sales letters, information packets and handouts.

A news release must be newsworthy. With this in mind, consider all the things your firm is doing that others might find of interest. Do you have results of an annual survey or customer opinion poll? Did you recently receive a large order or are you hiring additional people? Have you developed a new product or process? Are you now selling to an overseas market?

When writing a news (media) release, follow established guidelines, but be creative:

- Use standard-size 8½" x 11" paper.
- At the top, type the date and FOR IMMEDIATE RELEASE (or the release date).
- List your firm's name, address, phone number and the name of the person in your organization to contact for additional information.
- Include a headline in capital letters that tells the reader what the news release is about, and why it is important.
- Double-space the copy.
- The first paragraph should contain a summary of this mini-article.
- Think of your news release copy as a pyramid. The most valuable information is placed at the top, followed by less valuable information in descending order.
- Write in your finest Sgt. Joe Friday style, "nothing but the facts." If opinions or results of a survey are included, place them in quotes.
- Answer the questions that readers ask: Who? What? When? Where? Why?
- Conclude the release with ##### centered at the copy's end.

To give your news release proper publicity, compile a mailing list of the media in your area. Within one hour, you can have the names you need. For example, if your news release is business-related, list the names of all business editors for your area's newspapers. Then list the names of the news directors at local radio stations and the assignment editors at television stations.

These names can be entered into your computer or typed on a master so they can be duplicated on "3 up" mailing labels on your copy machine. You will find that the easier it is to send a news release, the more you will send. News releases increase your chances of getting free publicity and new customers.

If you're creative, there are many other ways to attract free media attention, without using a news release. A refuse company drew national media attention when they sent a garbage truck to the twentieth anniversary celebration of Woodstock. The firm saw a way to capitalize on the mounds of garbage that were left there 20 years earlier.

Your daily paper usually has several examples of how firms in your area used a little creativity to get free publicity. If you think an idea will work, try it — what do you have to lose?

20. Publish a Newsletter

Customer-oriented newsletters are not only a cost-effective way to stay in touch with current customers, they are a great way to interest new ones. Newsletters can lure new customers in two ways: First, you can include your referral message, "If you're happy with us, please tell others." Secondly, it can be used as a low-cost direct mail tool because people will read and keep a newsletter that they feel contains valuable information.

_____

Given a Choice
We Would All
Rather Do Business
With Friends

_____

Your newsletter can be simple and effective. The copy should contain information that is beneficial to your average customer. Explain how one of your products or services is helping customers to solve problems. Subscribe to the same magazines and trade journals as your customers. Awareness of the type of information they are looking for will provide you with more than enough information for a quarterly newsletter. After collecting the information, simply rewrite the material and cut and paste it in column form on your newsletter board.

Design a distinctive masthead, or have a graphic artist design it for you. Your local trade/technical school may have a graphic design department that would be glad to provide several ideas from which to choose. A quick printer can typeset the masthead with your name, phone number, etc., usually for under $80.

You can start with something as simple as a two-sided 8½" x 11" newsletter. Surprisingly, a quality image can be maintained at a very reasonable cost.

21. Become an Authority

According to Webster's Dictionary, an authority is "someone who has much knowledge or experience in some field and whose opinion is reliable." If you have been in business more than two years by definition, aren't you an authority?

The secret is to let the media find out that you are an authority. Start with your local newspaper. Contact the editors of the news and feature sections that your customers read. For example, if you specialize in accounting services, send a letter to the business editor and follow up with a call. Describe how you can help that section. Mention the biggest problem currently being faced by your clients, or show the results of your annual business forecast, customer opinion poll or survey of local civic leaders.

You may be able to give the editor a story idea. Subtly offer your services as being knowledgeable in that area, should the need ever arise. Use your magazine and newsletter articles to help support your position. Few things will give you (and your firm) more credibility than to be quoted as an expert in a newspaper story.

Follow the same procedure with radio talk show program directors and television assignment editors. You may be pleasantly surprised when you receive a call saying, "We've been looking for someone to discuss that problem for a long time." To obtain the name and title of the person to contact, call your local talk radio stations, television stations and newspapers — usually the receptionist is glad to help.

22. *Exhibit at Trade Shows*

Depending on your product or service, trade shows can generate a large number of qualified leads at a fairly low cost per lead (CPL). The key is to select a trade show or exhibit that the decision makers in your target market attend. Booth space may range from $100 to over $1,500, but can pay for itself many times over in sales to new customers.

Planning is paramount. It may be wise to send a letter or postcard inviting promising target customers to attend the show and to visit your booth. Establish goals, such as the number of leads you will generate or sales you will make. Your objective should be to establish personal contact with future customers.

Be prepared. Have your booth manned by at least three people during the "prime exhibit time." Your people should be on their feet, enthusiastic and ready to go out of their way to introduce themselves and your company. Provide literature with your name and phone number for visitors who don't have time to speak to one of your sales staff.

During the show, check progress every hour and make necessary changes immediately. Attract attention, inform, and entertain. Consider setting up a slide projector with an automatic timer that shows your current customers using and enjoying your product or service.

Create excitement. Ask the manufacturer or distributor of your products for a demonstration model, "cut-away" or other presentation materials which you can use in your booth. Consider having signs made for the back of your booth that list the benefits your firm offers your customers.

Drawing a business card from a fishbowl for a valuable prize may be hokey, but it works. Before placing a prospect's card in the fishbowl, note any important information or follow-up required on its back. For extra mileage, ask the president of the trade association hosting the trade show to draw the business card(s). Be prepared to take several pictures with a good quality camera. Submit the best photos and a news release listing the winners to the trade association for publication in their next newsletter or magazine.

To determine which trade shows and product exhibitions are right for your firm, ask your librarian for copies of trade show schedules, exhibit directories and convention guides.

If you feel you can't afford the booth rental, consider sharing the cost with another business that complements yours. Don't forget to ask the manufacturer of the products you sell to provide co-op funds.

23. Use the Yellow Pages Wisely

For many businesses, the Yellow Pages can be a good source of leads but, unfortunately, many others annually waste thousands of dollars on Yellow Pages advertising. The effectiveness of telephone directory advertising is determined by several factors:

- Size of the ad. Large ads usually are read before smaller ones, but just because an ad is read doesn't mean it will generate a call.

- When several of your area's businesses have large Yellow Pages ads but use an answering machine or their phone has been disconnected, some consumers could form a negative opinion about all advertisers with large ads.

- Your ad should be the same size as those displayed by the four or five firms who form your true competition.

- Ad location is important. A telephone directory's index may include several headings where your message could be appropriate. You must determine which heading potential customers will check first. Ads located in a position where they won't be seen are a waste of money. Do some research and ask several people which heading they would look under for your firm's products/services.

- Positioning is more than being first in a particular listing, as positioning creates an image of your company in a potential customer's mind. To help create a positive image of professionalism, use the logos of trade associations to which you belong. If you have been in business several years, let people know it. Also, display the logos of any credit cards you honor.

- To save money and still get results, consider placing an inexpensive "in-column" ad under all of the logos or brand names of the products you sell or service.

- Make your ad stand out. Use a headline. If everyone else has used black and white ads, use red; the higher cost is usually justified. Ad copy must be strong — it should differentiate you from your competition, answer the questions most people have and convince the reader that they should call you first.

- Consider offering something free in your ad. An appliance store offers a free booklet on things to check before calling for service.

- Many people using the Yellow Pages do so to shop price. If your firm sells value instead of price, it may be wise for you to inform the public about your company through additional sources.

- Learn from your toughest competitors' strengths and mistakes — study their ads. Chances are, that firms that have been in business several years know what approach gets results for their business and their competitors.

A Yellow Pages' ad is a long-term investment. In most cases you have to pay for it every month, whether you receive any calls or not. Unlike many forms of advertising, an ad placed there does not create desire for your product or service, it only directs people who have already decided to buy. Investigate all alternatives before you invest. The Yellow Pages may work for you, but it should only be one element of your plan to acquire new customers.

For Many Businesses the Yellow Pages Can Be a Good Source of Leads... Unfortunately Others Annually Waste Thousands of Dollars on Yellow Pages Advertising

24. Host a Tour or Open House

People are naturally curious. If you let them view your operation from the inside, they will have a better understanding of your company. Understanding leads to trust, and trust leads to sales.

Any business can host a tour or open house. Your motivation is simply a desire to show your potential customers why they should do business with you. This also can be tied into a new product or special promotion. Flyers sent to your target customers and a supply of snack foods may be your total expense.

Consider inviting your mayor, district senator or representative, industry opinion leaders and local celebrities. Be prepared for photo opportunities. A few well-selected photographs can provide you with substantial material for several press releases.

Tours work great, especially if you make, process or design something. They can be equally effective for firms such as florist shops, sheet metal shops and data processing companies. If possible, show the process from start to finish. One eye surgeon recently combined a tour of his facility with an actual operation so prospective patients could see a new procedure to correct near-sightedness firsthand.

Ask your prospect's accounting people to tour with your accounting staff. If you have a technical product, invite technical people from your prospect's firm. Relationships established on these levels make future sales much easier.

If used properly, a side benefit of tours and open houses can be increased employee morale. Get everyone involved in sharpening up your facility's appearance. If the tour provides the results you wanted, make it an annual focal point in your plan to obtain new customers.

25. Conduct Seminars

People want information on ways to make their lives better. Many are willing to attend a seminar, if they can see how it will directly benefit them.

Seminars can be a great way for you to simultaneously provide up-to-date information to several prospects. Some businesses that routinely host seminars include: accounting firms, real estate brokers, insurance agencies and financial planners. Additionally, seminars can attract new customers if your product or service requires a major purchasing decision, customer education, or if changes in laws or product designs affect current or potential customers.

Many benefits result from utilizing seminars to develop new customers. Since you have attracted several prospects to one location, you have reduced the number of sales calls you would have to make. If you figure that the average face-to-face sales call costs over $250, seminars are extremely cost-effective. Seminars also provide more credibility than sales calls. You can demonstrate your knowledge and show that you are not afraid to answer the audience's questions. Your showmanship in a seminar will get people more emotionally involved than if you approached them one-on-one in an office setting with normal daily distractions. Simply said, a group will give you a highly charged environment to showcase your products/services.

Many newspapers and magazines include a listing of upcoming seminars. A news release addressed to the business editor is all that is necessary. If you can make your seminar newsworthy enough, you may be able to obtain free public service spots on one or more radio stations. You also can use direct mail, print advertising and other methods for attracting the attention of potential clients.

The seminar should be offered free or at very low cost. If you feature a celebrity or recognized expert as a speaker, you can charge more. One to two hours usually provides enough time to present your message without your audience becoming bored. Spend at least 80 percent of the time covering useful information and questions and answers. The last few minutes should be used to "ask for the order." With a well-chosen list of prospects, you should be able to close 10 percent to over 20 percent of the participants. With post-seminar follow up, your closing rate could be much higher.

26. Take Advantage of Small Space Advertising

Many times, less is more. According to the Newspaper Advertising Bureau, at least seven out of 10 families read the classified advertising in their daily paper. Six out of the same 10 buy from those who make their offer in the classifieds. A classified ad has several advantages:

- It is easy to prepare.
- It is simple to start and stop — just pick up the phone.
- You can test several messages before you invest in a display ad.
- With some creativity, it will be read by serious buyers.

Some ideas to consider when placing a classified ad:

- Consider placing an ad in all of the magazines and newspapers that your target customers read.
- Make your ad large enough to include all of the important details. Limit the use of abbreviations.
- Differentiate your ad from others.
- Try a classified display ad where you can use a reverse (white type on black background), border, bold print, oversized or all capital letters, etc.

• Plan on running your ad for several weeks while you track results.

After you have determined which classified ad is your best, consider using it as a foundation on which to build a small space display ad. Because repetition is critical in advertising, eight 1/8-page display ads will usually outdraw a one-time full-page ad. Look into having the ad placed adjacent to the editorial copy of a popular columnist once or twice per week. Such placement can increase its effectiveness.

27. Make the Most of Zone Ads

National newspaper and magazine zone ads offer the power and prestige of a large publication for the fraction of what it would cost if you advertised nationally. For example, *Time* magazine has many editions that are broken down by state and large cities. Nationally published newspapers like *The Wall Street Journal* and *USA Today* have regional editions. Even most large city newspapers have zone editions which appeal to readers from a specific geographical area.

Many people equate ads in national publications with credibility. After your ad runs in a zone edition of a prestigious journal or publication, you can use the now famous, "as seen in . . ." in your other advertising. Also several large publications utilize a self-mailer response card which makes it simple for the readers who are interested in your offer to request additional information from your firm.

If there is a zone edition of a large newspaper and local newspaper serving the same area, you can run a test ad in both publications. Use a coupon with different offers printed in both papers on the same day. Track results until you know which provides the most new customers for the lowest cost.

For any publication you consider using this form of advertising in, locate the name and phone number of your area's advertising manager in the periodical's masthead (situated in the front portion of any magazine/ publication).

Some things to consider when placing a print ad:

- The first goal of your ad is to grab the reader's attention.
- Focus on the benefits your customer will receive, not your product/service.
- Have a professional graphic artist design your ad. (A well-designed ad can be reproduced in several sizes and used in flyers, postcards, posters, etc.)
- Copy must make the ad stand out from the others.
- Give the reader a reason to act.
- Keep the ad simple. Avoid clutter.
- Consider placing a window in your ad to insert special offer.
- It may take at least three months to test an ad's effectiveness.
- A good ad's life can be two years or longer.

28. Consider "Shopper" and Weekly Newspaper Ads

In many areas, the publications that are distributed free to consumers are called Shoppers. Most are loaded with ads for local businesses. The good news is that advertisements are usually inexpensive to run and can attract high readership. The bad news is that many people reading these ads are bargain hunters and may

_____

People Don't Buy
Your Product or Service
For What It Is. . .

They Buy It
For What It Does
Specifically For Them

_____

not be interested in top-of-the-line merchandise or added value. Before placing an ad here, determine if you have a unique product or are willing to compete with a low-price competitor.

If your product lends itself well to this type of publication, try advertising there. Because of the fairly low cost, place an ad that dominates the page. You may save additional money by obtaining ad copy from your product's manufacturer. By tracking your results, you can determine if you have found another low-cost method to reach new customers.

29. *Utilize Directories and Newsletters*

Almost every club, trade association, civic organization, school and church has a directory or newsletter, and many include advertising. Depending on the organization, you may find that many of your target customers use their directory when making a purchasing decision. Response from directories can range from zip to encouraging, depending on how many members need and can afford your product or service. Given a choice, members prefer dealing with other members.

Consider using the directories for the organizations to which you belong. If your goal is to support your club or organization, and to inform your fellow members of your offer, then this is the place.

If one of the organizations to which you or your target customer belongs has a newsletter that includes advertising, try placing an ad there. Compared to magazines and newspapers, newsletters have a very limited readership, but those who receive it read it and may save it for a long time. Since newsletter ads usually cost next to nothing, the odds may be in your favor of attracting new customers at a very low cost.

30. Make the Most of Bulletin Boards

Bulletin boards are such an obvious way to get sales messages to new customers they are often overlooked. They are not simply used for advertising baby-sitting and lawn care service. It's not uncommon to find everything from well-known accounting services to nationally published business and financial newspapers advertised on bulletin boards.

Large bulletin boards, like those found in many grocery stores and shopping centers, may contain pockets or trays where you can place your flyers or brochures. If there are no pockets, staple your material to the board and attach several cards containing your firm's name and phone number. Your printer can perforate your cards so interested individuals can easily tear one off and call you later. Bulletin boards may be located in laundromats, apartment complex laundry rooms, community centers, banks, churches, etc. Look for them as you do your daily errands.

As with other ad copy, make yours stand out from all of the other material displayed. Consider two-color printing, an action photograph or attention-getting headline. Identify all of the bulletin boards in your trade area. Assign an entry level employee, such as a delivery person, to check and routinely replenish supplies.

31. Profit from Co-Op Ads

Free money for advertising? At least part of your ad may be paid for by others. A large number of manufacturers make co-op funds available to their dealers, if they are mentioned in your ads.

The most successful way to get co-op funds is to ask for them. Talk to each of your suppliers. Federal law mandates that a supplier must make equal co-op offers to all of their customers, but they don't have to tell you about it. Over $2.5 billion in co-op dollars was unclaimed in 1986 alone.

To help defray your advertising expenses, some manufacturers offer camera-ready artwork, literature, and other marketing materials available at no cost.

You may be able to obtain co-op funds from more than one source for the same ad. This enables you to reach out to new customers at a greatly reduced cost. Whenever you advertise, ask yourself, "Who can I get to share the costs?"

Another form of co-op or shared-cost advertising is to advertise with non-competitors. This can be accomplished in several ways. First, consider advertising with businesses physically close to yours. If you own a dress shop, contact the shoe and jewelry stores located next door to you.

An additional way to advertise with non-competitors is through use of direct-response cards. These cards are a collection of postcards from several businesses that are packaged together and sent to specific target markets. Each advertiser has one or more cards with the product information printed on the front and their return address on the back. Interested readers simply fill out the card and return it to your firm. The cost of these cards can be as low as 3 cents a piece. The market that these cards reach and other important information is listed in the Standard Rate and Data Service book entitled _Card Deck Rates and Data_ located in your library. For additional information on several different types of mailing pack programs, look under "Advertising" in the Yellow Pages.

32. Use Signs Effectively

If your store or place of business is located on a busy street, over 40,000 potential customers could be driving by every day. A well-placed sign can turn drive-bys into new customers. To determine the traffic count in front of your firm, call your city's traffic engineer.

A sign is worthless unless it is seen. Unfortunately, most people tune out things they routinely see every day. The key is to break your future customer's preoccupation. See if any of the following tips might work for your sign:

• If it's lighted, consider having it flash.
• Leave your sign's lights on one day a week.
• Turn the light off one night per week.
• Do something that creates change. Weigh the possibility of covering your sign two days per month. People will wonder what's going on and you'll attract their attention.
• If you can change the message on your sign, do it often.
• Rotate your "specials."
• Use your sign to educate.
• Use humor (this may not work for a mortuary).
• Tell people why they should do business with you.
• Explain how you'll solve their problems.
• Other ways to gain attention at a low cost are through the use of pennants, banners, and flags.
• If you are going to replace or install a sign, consider one that rotates. Movement will subconsciously draw people's attention (an instinct from the caveman days).

Consider the possibility of placing a bus bench with your message in front of your facility. Because bus benches are close to the street and at eye level, they are easily seen.

Think about renting a lighted, movable sign. If you're not located on a busy street, can you place it at a busy intersection? Look for a trade-off. For instance, you may be able to trade storage space at your facility to a firm that has a window on a busy street where you can set up your sign.

Depending upon the type of business you own, a yard sign may be a fantastic opportunity to attract new customers at no cost. Work that is performed at a home or business that requires more than one day to complete is ideal for utilizing yard signs. An example is, "This New Roof Is Being Professionally Installed by XYZ Co. Call 123-3333 for a Free Estimate." Not only will many people driving by see your sign, you will have established instant credibility because one of their neighbors obviously trusts you. Additionally, as in the case of the new roof, other houses in that neighborhood are probably the same age and also in need of a new roof.

If you have a delivery truck or service vehicles, make sure they all have signs. If everything else is equal, choose a van over a pickup truck. Vans provide a large space for your company's name and message, it can become a fantastic movable billboard.

If you are located in a city with several high-rise buildings, consider painting your firm's name on top of your vehicles so they can be seen. If you have a large fleet, use the same signs and paint color on all vehicles. Your vehicles will appear to be everywhere.

Being visible is one way to gain a place in your future customers' minds. When they have a need for the product or service that you provide, you're the one who is likely to be called.

33. *Employ Displays and Demonstrations*

If a picture is worth 1,000 words, then a display is worth a million and a demonstration speaks volumes. Window displays can attract new customers at a very low cost. They should be attractive, draw people to them and should be changed often. If you currently don't have a window display, take a critical look at your business. How much trouble would it be to modify your facility to incorporate a window display? The time and money spent may be easily recaptured in increased revenue from new customers. If a window display won't work, can you effectively use a window sign?

Consider a floor display. If you sell something mechanical, such as lawn mowers or washing machines, check out the possibilities of getting a cutaway model from the manufacturer. This type of display can function as your biggest sales aid.

If you have a product that can be demonstrated, such as a new fax machine or food processor, make sure your entire sales staff knows how it operates and understands all of its features, advantages and benefits.

The biggest mistakes made when performing a demonstration are not telling the prospect what to expect before the demonstration, and not asking how the product could help solve the customer's current problem upon completion.

Depending on your type of business, consider putting a display in a shopping mall during a well-publicized event. If the number of new customers you obtain warrants it, get a short-term lease on a kiosk (space in the center of the mall). If that approach works out you may be ready for a permanent second location in the mall.

34. *Deliver Top Quality Service*

The most important difference between you and your competition is the quality of your service. The goal of top-quality service is total customer satisfaction. When your customers are happy they will tell others about you. Positive word-of-mouth advertising is vital to the success of any business which wants additional customers.

Because every customer encounter is critical, everyone in your organization from the receptionist to the CEO must be committed to quality and must understand his/her role in customer satisfaction. Ultimately, the owner and managers determine the level of quality. Intentional or not, they lead through example. Industry leaders know that if they give "lip service" to quality and then place real emphasis on "profitability at any cost," they will lose current customers and will fail to attract new ones.

Data shows that some companies spend up to 40 percent of their time making mistakes. People will forgive mistakes if they are immediately corrected by people who care. Quality service doesn't just happen, it requires planning. Answers to the following questions should be incorporated into your 12-month plan to attract new customers.

- What level of service are we willing to provide?
- How can the current level of quality be improved?
- How will we know when quality is excellent or poor?
- What constitutes acceptable behavior of our employees?
- Who will be responsible for the management of quality?

Make it easy for customers to provide feedback on the level of service quality your organization provides. Con-

---

The Most Important Difference Between You and Your Competition is the Quality of Your Service

---

sideration should be given to providing customer response cards or a phone call after a purchase is made or service is completed.

The benefits of top quality service include:

• Greater customer loyalty
• More referrals
• Repeat purchases
• Lower sales/marketing costs
• Higher profit margins without losing customers

In the final analysis, it is not how good *you* think the service is, it is what *your customer* thinks that counts. It's easy to see how total customer satisfaction can be the key to increased profitability. To grow and prosper top-quality service isn't an option, it's a requirement.

35. Sell Profit Improvement

The one common language of all foreign or domestic businesses is MONEY. Whatever your product or service, determine how it saves people money or improves their "bottom line." For instance, using a certain type of material results in a new suit lasting twice as long. That saves money. An air conditioning unit can be replaced with a new one that only requires two-thirds as much electricity. This can provide a 20 percent return on investment by reducing the electric bill. A certain brand of copy machine uses an inexpensive toner and dry ink. Over time, the owner will save hundreds of dollars in re-occurring supply costs.

Today's consumers are bombarded with a barrage of choices. Your objective is to be selected from that crowd. Selling profit improvement in a manner that demonstrates direct benefits to your prospects eliminates competition that offers only goods and services.

Take a critical look at your products and services. How can they save your customers money or improve their profits? When a prospect says "Your price is too high," you will be able to demonstrate that the profit improvement you offer is their best value.

36. Sell Added Value

Value is what your current and future customers are willing to pay for your product or service. Value is determined by the benefits they receive — more benefits create higher value. People only buy when value exceeds the price. The firm that provides the most wanted, needed or desired benefits at a realistic cost gains new customers.

In most cases, the value your future customers receive is more important than the price they pay. Less than 20 percent of our nation's consumers buy the lowest priced product/service without comparing what benefits that purchase provides. Only when value appears to be equal do people buy the lowest priced product/service.

People want different things from the same product or service. The secret to selling value is to understand what your customers consider valuable. A large percentage may purchase from your firm because your warranty or exchange policy eliminated their fears and doubts. Others may patronize your company because of your quality service, quick delivery, or convenient business hours. Find out why your customers buy from you by asking them. Once you find out what is valuable to them, use this information in your advertising, promotion, and lead generation plan to attract new customers.

You can create value several ways. Value increases with demand. When future customers learn how they will get the added benefits they desire from your product/ service, demand increases. When you offer a unique product/service that people like, value increases.

When costs are reduced through smarter buying, reduced transportation expense or lower overhead, you can reduce your price and increase value. If your competitor offers a 90-day warranty and yours is for 180 days you've increased your product's value.

Develop a list of all the ways your firm can create more value with the products/services you currently are selling. To help with this important task consider the following:

- Value, like quality, is what your customers say it is. Perception is reality.
- People don't buy what your product/service is, but what it does for them.
- Discover what is valuable to your prospects and wrap your message around it.
- Focus on non-price issues.
- Explain how your product or service is unique.
- Stress your firm's superior product knowledge.
- Explain how your prospects will gain something: revenue, comfort, peace of mind, dependability, personal service, etc.
- Tell how you will reduce the potential for loss. (Fear of loss can be greater than desire for gain.)
- Provide only enough facts to show value, don't overwhelm prospects with too much information. Every fact must have a related benefit which is important to your prospect.
- Be able to prove the value of your benefits by using test results, testimonials, or other hard evidence.

All things being equal, the company that provides the greatest value gains the most new customers.

37. *Provide Convenience*

Americans will do business with those firms providing convenience. This is evidenced by the number of "convenience" stores that dot almost every major intersection in cities throughout the United States. For many Americans, their time is more important than the added cost they know they pay for convenience.

Convenience is anything that contributes to a person's comfort or makes their lives or work easier. Consider the following:

* The average person spends more time than ever commuting to and from work
* Both husbands and wives work in approximately 50 percent of today's marriages. By the year 2000, 75 percent of all married couples will be working
* Working mothers are putting in more hours as their children grow up
* By 1995, 65 percent of all new mothers will be working outside of the home.

Obviously the traditional business hours of 9:00 A.M. to 5:00 P.M. may be anything but convenient. One of the most overlooked ways to provide convenience is to make the benefits of your business available to future customers when it's the easiest for them to buy.

Can you change or modify your business hours to suit your current and future customers' needs? How about opening earlier, closing later, staying open all day Saturday, Sunday or on holidays?

If people can't come to you, can you go to them? Many retail businesses have become mobile. Everything from shoe repair to office equipment showrooms are now on wheels. (The new motor home you've wanted could become a legitimate business expense.)

Americans Will Do Business With Firms Who Provide Convenience

Many firms that have been providing service in homes and offices for years are now providing more convenience. Employee work hours are staggered so they can provide service from 6:00 A.M. to 8:00 P.M. without charging for overtime. Employees of some firms gladly work weekends so they can have days off during the week when recreational areas and entertainment facilities are less crowded.

The key to offering convenience is to know and understand what convenience means to your current and future customers. A well-planned telephone survey of a percentage of your current customers should reveal what convenience means to them. At the same time, you should be able to gather other valuable information that can be used to acquire new customers.

38. Sell Customized Solutions

A customized solution is a package made up of one or more of your firm's related products or services. The process starts by analyzing your customer's most pressing problems. Fact finding must be done first because *prescription before diagnosis is malpractice.* List all of the elements that are needed to form your customized solution.

One automotive repair shop that specializes in brake repair customizes a solution which meets more than their customer's need for new brakes. Besides providing pickup and delivery from their customer's home or office they also wash the car and perform routine maintenance (e.g., tire rotation, checking of fluids and belts) before the car is returned.

A fast-growing computer store knows how to sell customized solutions. It not only sells computers, it also provides a basic software package. One of the firm's employees sets up the computer in the customer's home or office then spends at least an hour explaining how to start using the computer. The employee calls one week following installation to answer any questions then sends a list of training programs and computer-user clubs located in their new customer's area.

The sales price of a customized solution must be determined by all of the benefits your new customers will receive. The more benefits you provide, the more value you add. Factors such as convenience, high quality, profit improvement, comfort, better health, peace of mind and more free time can increase your selling price and profit margins.

Be creative. Study all of the products and services you sell. How can you position them as customized solutions to solve future customers' problems?

39. Put the Law of Reciprocity to Work for You

Not that many years ago, when a farmer needed a barn built, the entire community joined together and had it completed in a day. When the next farmer needed a new barn, the first workers to arrive were those who had already benefitted from a barn raising. Aside from frontier spirit, one reason people showed up was the law of reciprocity. When someone does something kind or beneficial for you, you feel morally obligated to return "like kind" behavior.

With this in mind, examine all of the firms from which you and your company purchase. If you offer a product or service they need and they aren't buying it from you, ask them why.

The owner of a carpet-cleaning company used this strategy quite effectively. She met with the manager of her bank and after pointing out two or three problem areas with the carpets and explaining the benefits of having her firm routinely clean them, she requested an opportunity to demonstrate what her firm could do. The manager gave his stock answer that another firm was already cleaning the carpets. The owner's reply was simple, "Do they have their personal and business checking and savings accounts with your branch?"

After showing the manager what a great job her firm could do at the branch, the manager willingly referred the owner to the bank's property management division. Within six months, the owner of the carpet cleaning service had 36 bank branches as customers. She simply used the law of reciprocity to get her foot in the door and her quality service created the necessary momentum.

40. Provide Financing

Many consumers can't spend $1,000 but can afford $10 per week. Compared to our major competitors, Americans don't save much money. The Japanese save over 18 percent of their gross national product. The West Germans save over 10 percent. Americans save less than 3 percent. To make matters worse, the Tax Reform Act of 1986 strongly discourages business and individual savings. Providing financing may be one way to attract new customers who want what you're selling but don't have the ready cash to buy it.

Financing comes in many forms. The most common form is credit cards. There are over 725 million credit cards in the hands of approximately 105 million Americans. The average consumer has several thousand dollars worth of credit in her purse or his wallet. Occasionally, they must be reminded that their buying power is immediately available.

One obvious, yet sometimes overlooked, source of financing is your bank. With a small investment in time, you and your employees will be instructed on how to fill out various loan applications and understand the applicable truth-in-lending laws.

If you sell a large ticket item, the manufacturer or distributor may offer financing, occasionally at a reduced rate. Your local utility company also may have a financing program for certain items such as appliances or energy-related products.

Should your resources support it, consider providing your own financing. There is a risk, but you will get new sales and revenue from the interest that otherwise you would have missed.

Inform people through your advertising and lead generation materials that financing is available. All things being equal, the firm with financing will attract the new customers.

41. Barter

The United States' free enterprise system was founded on the concept of barter — exchanging goods and services without using money. Many business people enjoy bartering, but rarely do it because today's business climate is supposed to be too sophisticated for that. The truth is, given a chance, a lot of people are willing to barter. The secret is to ask.

If you provide a service that a newspaper, magazine, radio or television station routinely needs, try bartering.

59

For example, an air conditioning service company may be able to trade an air conditioning and heating equipment preventive maintenance program for a daily 60-second radio advertisement during the morning drive time. An accounting firm provides bookkeeping services for a local magazine in exchange for a full-page ad every month. A clothing store provides a new suit for a television station's reporter, in exchange for a credit at the end of the news broadcast. (Remember to keep proper records for tax purposes.)

Using the local radio station for another example, radio stations conduct many contests and the on-air personality may mention your firm if you provide a prize (e.g., offer a dinner for two at your restaurant, a watch from your jewelry store, an automotive repair service from your garage, or a pair of hard to get tickets for a sports event). Additionally, you may be able to use a combination of paid advertising and barter to greatly extend your advertising dollars.

Remember, to barter, all you have to do is ask. The worst that could happen is the business person will say no.

42. Negotiate

Negotiation is a process of reaching agreement. Almost everything is negotiable. Unlike barter, you are willing to exchange money to advertise and generate leads, but you want to pay less or gain more favorable terms.

Print advertising may be negotiated in several ways. If time is on your side, let the advertising manager know it. You may be able to negotiate a good price by letting the manager hold your ad and insert it in the publications he or she needs material for, or for when there is a last-minute cancellation. You also may be able to negotiate a per inquiry (P.I.) or per order (P.O.) agreement. Using this arrangement, you acquire advertising space with no up-front cost. You simply pay an agreed upon amount for each inquiry or order you generate from the ad. When negotiating for a P.I., P.O. or other arrangement, explain all of the ways the advertising manager and his/her publication will benefit. A few things to keep in mind when negotiating include:

- Know what you want in advance.
- Learn as much as possible about the media with which you are dealing. Know their ad rates (available at your library), their slow and busy seasons, etc.
- If possible, negotiate in person
- Ask for more than you are willing to accept
- Explain the value of the product/service you are negotiating in dollars and cents.
- Time is money. If you have the time to wait for your advertising to run, you can save money.

The secret to successful negotiations is that both sides attain what they want.

43. Provide a Free Consultation

In many service businesses, a leading way to win new customers is to demonstrate what you can do for them. A free consultation is the ultimate free sample.

A free consultation provides an opportunity to establish rapport. Rapport is one element that helps turn prospects into customers. It's much easier to establish rapport when you're working with your customer as a consultant rather than as a salesman. A free consultation also offers opportunities to discover specific needs. Once you know your future customer's needs, you can tailor a solution to solve his or her problems, at your normal fee. You both win. You have made your newest customer's life better and you have acquired a revenue-producing customer (client).

The secret to providing a free consultation is not to divulge all of your knowledge. In many cases, one-half hour to two hours should be ample time to conduct a preliminary fact finding and needs analysis. Consider providing an invoice for your time and mark it "no charge," so your prospect is made aware of the value of your time. Follow up with a meeting and state the benefits you can provide the client by completing the work you've already started.

44. *Offer a Free Second Opinion*

When a person has been diagnosed as having a serious illness, he will probably get a second opinion from another doctor. If your firm provides a service, you may benefit by offering potential customers a second opinion at no cost or obligation.

Your cost in providing a free second opinion may be the least expensive marketing you will ever do. Many times your firm will be the last one to see the prospect's problem and offer a solution. The last firm always has an advantage. People easily tire of dealing with problems, so if you offer to remove that problem at a fair cost, you probably have a new customer. Occasionally, you may discover the problem was misdiagnosed and you can be the one to provide the good news. This action will gain a customer's trust and places you in a strong position to get future business and referrals.

Your free second opinion message should be listed in your advertising as it will distinguish you from your competition.

Any time you can illustrate your firm's uniqueness to potential customers, the value of your advertising message increases.

45. *Give a Free Sample to Opinion Leaders*

Sometimes in order to sell it, you have to give it away first. Many successful businesses were started by the founder giving samples to prospective customers. People won't buy what they don't know they're missing. By giving samples to a select few, you may be able to use this technique even for your firm's more costly products or services.

Think leverage. Ask yourself how you can attain the greatest return on a free sample investment? Start by thinking about who you can give a sample to that will tell others. If you own a restaurant, give a free dinner to employees of the beauty or barber shops nearby. If you provide a good meal and treat these folks as VIPs they probably will tell many of their customers about your restaurant and their pleasant experience.

Your free sample can be expensive, if the investment warrants it. A cruise ship line probably wouldn't hesitate to give a one-week cruise to the owner of a large travel agency, because this person is in a position to refer hundreds of new customers.

Make a list of all the opinion leaders that warrant a free sample — respected members of your customers' trade associations, the minister of a large church, public officials, etc. Depending on your business, it may be worthwhile to contact the persons who received the samples to determine if he/she was totally satisfied. If they were satisfied, secure their permission to use their names when contacting other prospective customers.

If you offer small, new, unique or inexpensive products, consider providing them as samples. Many successful ice cream, cookie and office supply businesses were started and continued to grow because new customers received free samples. When giving a free sample, be sure to provide information on where new customers can purchase it.

46. Take Advantage of Cable TV

Television has to be one of the greatest places to advertise, but until recently most small businesses couldn't afford it. Cable television provides a low-cost opportunity to convince potential customers to give you their business. Ninety-seven percent of all American households have at least one television and it is turned on over seven hours per day. A large number of people who watch television will flip through the channels with their remote control when a commercial comes on. This practice is called grazing. Grazing provides an opportunity for your low-cost cable TV commercial to be watched by future customers.

For less than $500 you may be able to get a commercial produced that is suitable for cable television. A few things to consider when producing a quality, low-cost videotape for your commercial include:

• Shop for a video production company. In most large cities, you may be able to locate video production crews who "moonlight" or a good "cameraman" who has access to the necessary equipment.
• Contact your college or university media department.
• Do two or three commercials at the same time to reduce the cost further.
• Use one of your employees, but don't have them speak on camera.

Television
is One of the Greatest
Places to Advertise...

But Until Recently
Most Small Businesses
Couldn't Afford it

- Use a voice talent to do the soundtrack. Call a couple of radio stations and ask how much the on-air personalities charge to read a script.
- Show a problem, especially one of which many people are unaware, then demonstrate what happens if that problem isn't resolved.
- Entertain as well as inform.
- Constantly show your business name at the bottom of the screen during your spot. Even if the volume is off while the viewer is grazing, your firm's name will be noticed.
- Consider having one or two of your customers tell how happy they are with your products or services.
- Consider starring in your own commercial. Sincerity will gain credibility and new customers.
- Schedule your commercial so it will air during a network station break.
- Since the grazing viewer watches all stations, consider starting with an obscure cable station. You may be able to place your spot for a couple of dollars apiece, with a package deal.

47. Try Audiotapes

Have you ever received an unsolicited audiotape in the mail? Did you listen to it? Most people do. Since most people have audiotape players in their cars, this may be another low-cost way to get your message heard by promising target customers while they drive to work.

Start by "scripting" your message. Have it typed double-spaced, then contact a few firms listed in the Yellow Pages under "Audio-Visual Production Services." Tell them what you want to accomplish. You should be able to locate one firm who will do everything for you. Many firms work with local voice talents who can read your script. When a professional does this, the audiotape should have a much better "sound" and you'll save money on editing.

Secure a written quote before starting this project. Depending on the length and number of tapes you order, you should be able to produce a high-quality product that can attract new customers for less than $2 each.

48. Educate Your Customers

Astute people wouldn't think of passing up an opportunity to learn something new, especially if it will improve their lives or business. Educating future customers should be more than just a well-chosen tactic, it could be an integral part of your firm's marketing mission statement. "We will gain new customers by showing them how our services will improve their lives."

Many people have problems of which they are unaware. In this case, you will need to explain the problem, tell what will happen if it's not corrected, then explain why your firm should correct that problem now. For instance, a home owner who needs a new roof may not be aware that if a new one isn't installed in a timely manner, the rain and snow could damage the wood under the roofing and other parts of the home. The home owner could end up paying twice as much as necessary to repair the original problem.

When educating future customers:

• Physically show the problem to the prospect.
• Use photographs that illustrate problems.
• Show before and after shots.
• If possible, explain how much the uncorrected problem will cost in the future.
• Explain the cost of waiting.

67

• Build desire to have the problem solved.
• Paint vivid word pictures.
• Appeal to your prospect's logical needs.
• Appeal to your prospect's emotional needs.
• Explain what you have done for other customers.
• Use testimonials from satisfied customers.
• Use literature from your product's manufacturer to show how it is constructed or works.
• Explain all benefits the prospect will receive.

49. *Team Up With Your Research Librarian*

Would you like to have a consultant you could call on who would provide marketing research data and other information on ways to get new customers in your area? And as a bonus, no matter how much you used this expert's services you would never get a bill. If this sounds too good to be true, it's not — this remarkable consultant is your city's research librarian.

When you have a question or require specific information, all you have to do is call or visit your research librarian. Some of the tools he/she has available include:

• Standard Industrial Classification (SIC) code directories which categorize all businesses and assign each with a code which can be used when buying mailing lists and identifying future customers.
• Leads source books listing all businesses in your area and furnishing each one's SIC code.
• Publications that list new businesses in your area.
• Newspapers, local, regional and national magazines that can provide information about your best target customers and give you insight into market changes taking place which can benefit your firm.

- Corporate annual reports on firms in your area can demonstrate what your target customers need and explain changes that are taking place in personnel or corporate philosophy.
- *Directory of Corporations* will inform you of who the decision-makers are in many of your area's businesses.
- *Encyclopedia of Associations* lists associations that you may want to join to be more accessible to future customers.
- Standard Rate and Data Service publications provide a wealth of information including advertising rates and mailing lists' costs and availabilities.
- The *Trade Shows and Exhibits Schedule* lists schedules of trade shows in which you may decide to participate.
- The *Directory of Directories* provides local, state and national business information.
- There are also books on how to set up a direct mail program, how to save money on advertising, how to produce an effective brochure, how to write a business and marketing plan, and thousands more that can help you acquire new customers.

For best results, assign someone from your staff to meet with your reference librarian. Collect the data you will need to design a marketing program to help ensure your firm has a steady supply of new customers.

50. Provide a New Product / Service to Current Customers

Whether you sell an existing product to a new customer, or a new product to an existing customer, the results are the same, a "new" customer.

It's easy to understand why your best future customers are your current customers. They trust you because you

Your Best
Future Customers
Are Your
Current Customers

have eliminated doubt by doing what you say you will. An ongoing relationship with a customer is like Newton's law of motion ("a relationship in motion, tends to stay in motion"), so why not do something beneficial for both of you? Improve your customers' lives by providing additional products and services that complement those you are already offering. A florist delivering phone-in orders for a nearby pharmacy, or the clothing store that adds a line of luggage for their customers who travel on business are examples of this concept.

If adding a new product or service doesn't make sense, consider subcontracting one that your customers need. Many small construction-oriented firms routinely subcontract work on jobs that are too large for their work force. The firm's reward is the added benefit of extra revenue while retaining total control of their jobs. Their customers benefit because the firm they trust has assumed total responsibility for the project. Many people are willing to pay a little higher price for the convenience of single source responsibility and the opportunity to deal with those they already trust.

Your best future customers are your current customers.

51. Always Give More than Expected

If you had to rely on new customers every time you needed to make a sale, you would soon go broke. One of the greatest secrets to acquiring new customers is having your current ones return. Nothing works as well when creating customer loyalty, future business and golden referrals as exceeding your customers' expectations. Promise a lot in your advertising, promotion and lead generation, then deliver much more.

How to Obtain Results

Take a few moments to review this book. Study all of the ways listed to attract new customers. When you find an idea that you think will work for your firm, write it down, along with the date you will implement it, in the plan *How We Will Acquire New Customers*. Test your idea before investing large sums of money. Try to implement as many of the ideas outlined in this book as possible. Start with the simplest ones first, then when those are working well, add another. It's better to use seven or eight techniques well than 20 poorly. Think of this book as a smorgasbord of ideas. When you combine two or more ideas, their total becomes more powerful than each separate part.

The key to future growth and prosperity is the ability to obtain new customers at a reasonable cost. Knowledge, a small budget, and good intentions put into action are all it takes.

25 BENEFITS CUSTOMERS BUY

Record by percentage of importance the benefits
your most profitable customers want

- Style _____
- Value _____
- Health _____
- Safety _____
- Beauty _____
- Profits _____
- Comfort _____
- Service _____
- Quality _____
- Savings _____
- Prestige _____
- Pleasure _____
- Security _____
- Solutions _____
- Financing _____
- Knowledge _____
- Protection _____
- Acceptance _____
- Admiration _____
- Recognition _____
- Convenience _____
- Peace of Mind _____
- Dependability _____
- Relationships _____
- Personal Growth _____

15 KEYS TO ACQUIRING
NEW CUSTOMERS

1. BE NEW CUSTOMER ORIENTED
Every employee must understand their role in acquiring new customers.

2. BE ENTHUSIASTIC
Enthusiasm is the most powerful sales tool in history, and it's free.

3. BE PERSISTENT
Perseverance has won more new customers than the most expensive ad campaigns.

4. BE COMMITTED
Build strong relationships with your customers through care, friendship, and trust.

5. BE ALERT
Look for needs that people have which your competition has overlooked. Find a niche and fill it.

6. BE PERCEPTIVE
Find opportunities to acquire new customers before they become obvious to your competitors. (If you read about a new firm moving into your area it's too late.)

7. BE FLEXIBLE
Readily adapt proven new technology to make your current and future customers' lives better.

8. BE PREPARED
Take advantage of rapid changes caused by new laws, changing lifestyles, and unpredicted shifts in our economy.

9. **BE SELECTIVE**
   Dominate a segment of your market. When people have a need for your product/service, they will think of you.

10. **BE VISIBLE**
    Be there when your prospect discovers he has a need.

11. **BE UNIQUE**
    Demonstrate your individual strengths and distinguish your firm from your competitors.

12. **BE CREATIVE**
    Consumers are bombarded by hundreds of marketing messages every day, yours must stand out from the crowd.

13. **BE SHREWD**
    No matter how little an advertisement costs, if it doesn't attract new customers, it costs too much. Your goal is to get the best new customers at the lowest reasonable cost; be careful, but don't under-spend.

14. **BE PATIENT**
    Advertising, promotion and lead generation doesn't work immediately. One of the biggest mistakes is quitting too soon.

15. **BE CONSISTENT**
    Stick to your plan to acquire new customers. Constantly monitor results and be prepared to make necessary changes.

KNOW YOUR COMPANY

We are in the_____ business
(e.g., a book publisher is in the information business).

What we are really selling is _____
(the benefits your customers buy).

Our slogan is _____ (Describe
your firm's greatest asset and how it benefits your customers.)

Our greatest strengths are:

1. _____

2. _____

3. _____

4. _____

Our significant weaknesses are:

1. _____

2. _____

3. _____

We offer our customers these unique benefits:

1. _____

2. _____

3. _____

We can add these benefits at little or no cost:

1. _____

2. _____

What is likely to be different about business next year_____

_____

In three years?_____

How can we change what we are selling to take advantage of these
new opportunities? _____

_____

WHAT WORKED AND WHAT DIDN'T

Last year we spent $_____ on advertising,
promotion and lead generation.

Method	$ Amount	Number of Leads Generated
1. Yellow Pages		
2. Print Ads		
3. Radio Ads		
4. Television Ads		
5. Direct Mail		
6. Telemarketing		
7. Personal Sales Calls		
8. Trade Shows		
9. Bill Boards		
10. Bus Bench Advertising		
11. Flyers		
12. Signs		
13. Brochures		
14. Seminars		
15. Open House		
16.		

How can we change our current marketing message to attract more new customers? _____

How can we track the effectiveness of our new message? _____
_____

What new tools can we use to help educate our customers? ____
_____

PROSPECT DATA CARD

PROSPECT'S NAME _____

TITLE _____

PHONE NUMBER _____

ADDRESS _____

PROSPECT REPORTS TO _____

BIRTH DATE (day, not year)_____

PROFESSIONAL/TRADE ASSOCIATIONS _____

_____

IS CURRENTLY BUYING FROM _____

BECAUSE _____

GREATEST NEED IS _____

PERSONAL GOALS ARE_____

GREATEST ACHIEVEMENT IS _____

THE BEST WAY TO STAY IN TOUCH IS_____

THE BEST TIME TO CALL IS _____

THE BEST TIME TO MEET IS _____

ESTIMATED SALES, NEXT 12 MONTHS $_____

IMPORTANCE OF OUR PRODUCT/SERVICE   1 2 3 4 5 6 7 8 9 10

AMOUNT OF HASSLE INVOLVED   1 2 3 4 5 6 7 8 9 10

VALUE AS A POTENTIAL CUSTOMER   1 2 3 4 5 6 7 8 9 10

POTENTIAL FOR SOLID REFERRALS   1 2 3 4 5 6 7 8 9 10

PROBABILITY OF BECOMING A CUSTOMER   1 2 3 4 5 6 7 8 9 10

COMMENTS _____

_____

_____

_____

20 WAYS TO MAKE THE SALE

You are wasting your time and money if you can't turn a lead into a sale. The most common reasons prospects don't become customers is because: your price is higher than they were prepared to pay, your price is higher than your competitor's or the prospect didn't have enough information to desire your product or service. Until value has been established, your price is always too high.

1. **Explain that your price is only part of the final cost**
   - Prospect's time
   - Lost productivity
   - Unnecessary problems
   - Lost opportunities

2. **Discribe the cost of paying too little**
   - Poor quality
   - Short cuts
   - No warranty
   - Hidden costs
   - Longer completion time

3. **Gladly justify your higher price**
   - Highly skilled employees
   - Merchandise ready for immediate delivery
   - State-of-the-art products, processes and procedures
   - Professional management

4. **Spotlight your price**
   - "Our price only appears higher, but because of our resources we can do a better job at a lower total cost."

5. **Offer a warranty**
   - "We'll cover all parts and labor for one year"

6. Offer a Return on Investment
- "You will save enough on supplies to pay for it in less than five years."

7. Show that the benefits far out weigh the price
- "The increased productivity will increase your cash flow over $1000 per month."

8. Reduce the fear of loss
- "In the last five years we've saved our customers over a million dollars by eliminating common breakage."

9. Minimize the price difference
- "Our Service is only $30 a year more than you're paying now, that's less than 10 cents a day for all the extra benefits."

10. Break the price down
- "It will cost less than $2 per day"

11. Make it easy to buy
- "We can start with only 35% down and defer billing for 60 days."

12. Provide service
- "We'll respond in 3 hours or less, even on Christmas day."

13. Offer quality
- "Every time you see it you'll feel good about the quality we've added."

14. Question the price objection
- "Why do you think our price is too high? Do you mind if I ask how much too high?"

15. Sell your company's reputation
- "We have a reputation of honesty, quality and total customer satisfaction."

16. Verify that the prospect is making the right comparisons
- "Is XYZ Company also including muffler bearings and dyna-focal mounts in their price?"

17. Explain how the prospect loses if he doesn't buy
- "Because of the poor condition of your equipment, you are paying more than the price of our service in unnecessary utility costs."

18. Focus on what the prospect can earn
- "This program will increase your cash flow $250 per month."

19. Help the prosect arrange financing
- "If it will help, the manufacturer has both a leasing and financing program."

20. Sell yourself
- "When you become our customer, you also get me."

ACQUIRING YOUR COMPETITORS' CUSTOMERS

Which competitors have become complacent?

1. _____

2. _____

3. _____

4. _____

Which ones are not staying on top of changes in technology?

1. _____

2. _____

3. _____

4. _____

Which ones take their customers for granted?

1. _____

2. _____

3. _____

4. _____

Who are our competitors major customers?

1. _____

2. _____

3. _____

4. _____

5. _____

6. _____

7. _____

8. _____

How can we acquire our competitors' customers?

1. _____

2. _____

3. _____

4. _____

5. _____

Do we have the following competitors' information on file?

	Yes	No
• Yellow Pages ads	☐	☐
• Newspaper ads	☐	☐
• Radio ad script	☐	☐
• Television ad script	☐	☐
• Copy of news releases	☐	☐
• Newsletters	☐	☐
• Sales literature	☐	☐
• Contracts	☐	☐
• Proposals	☐	☐
• Annual report	☐	☐
• State Corporate filings	☐	☐
• Credit report	☐	☐

THE 9P's OF
MARKETING IN THE NEW ECONOMY

The goal of marketing is to create new customers
and keep current one's coming back

PEOPLE

The most critical element is your employees. If they
deliver more than your customers expect, your
customers will buy again and tell others about you.

PRODUCT

You must constantly be looking for innovative ways
to use new and existing products and services to
meet your current and future customers' ever
changing needs.

PRICE

When you are selling a "commodity" your price is
established by the market. But when you sell
solutions to problems, profit improvement and
customer satisfaction, your price is determined by
the value you provide.

PACKAGING

Packaging is attention to detail in everything from
letterhead design to making sure that everything
your customers see is spotless.

PROMOTION

Because the average company can lose over 20% of its customers every year, you must have an on-going advertisng, prmotion and lead generation program in order to grow and prosper.

POSITIONING

Differentiate your firm from your competition. Your goal is to help your future customers think of you when they have a need for your product or service.

PROFILE

To make every marketing dollar effective, you must have a profile of potential customers by profitability, expected future business, and the estimated number of referrals they can provide.

PLANNING

Without an on-going plan, new customers won't benefit from your products and services — you won't obtain new revenue — and marketing dollars will evaporate without a trace.

PERSONAL SALES

Face-to-face selling is an effective and costly marketing tool. It takes properly trained and motivated people to consistently turn prospects into customers.

KNOW YOUR CUSTOMERS

Our Best Customers	Why?	Common Traits They Share	Length of Time as Customer	Greatest Need
1.				
2.				
3.				
4.				
5.				
6.				
7.				
8.				
9.				
10.				
11.				
Problem Customers				
1.				
2.				
3.				
4.				
5.				
6.				
7.				
8.				
9.				
10.				
11.				

$ Volume 12 months	Why They Buy From Us	What Needs Are Changing	How Did They Hear About Us	Where They Live/Work

KNOW YOUR COMPETITION

Our Strongest Competitors	Why?	Strengths	Weaknesses
1. _____			
2. _____			
3. _____			
4. _____			
5. _____			
6. _____			
Our Weakest Competitors			
1. _____			
2. _____			
3. _____			
4. _____			
5. _____			
6. _____			
Anything competing for $ prospect would spend on our product/service			
1. _____			
2. _____			
3. _____			
4. _____			
5. _____			
6. _____			

Primary Marketing Methods	Where Ads Appear	Gain/Losing Market Share	Primary Benefits Offered

HOW WE WILL GET NEW CUSTOMERS
(A 12 Month Plan)

GOAL: Number of New Customers in Next 12 Months_____

Lead Generation Method	Annual Budget	WHEN METHOD WILL BE USED				
		Jan	Feb	Mar	Apr	May
1. _____	$					
2. _____	$					
3. _____	$					
4. _____	$					
5. _____	$					
6. _____	$					
7. _____	$					
8. _____	$					
9. _____	$					
10. _____	$					
11. _____	$					
12. _____	$					
13. _____	$					
14. _____	$					
15. _____	$					
16. _____	$					
17. _____	$					
18. _____	$					

TOTAL ANNUAL BUDGET $_____

WHEN METHOD WILL BE USED							True Cost	Number of New Customers	Cost/New Customer
Jun	July	Aug	Sept	Oct	Nov	Dec			

TOTAL COST $_____

TOTAL NUMBER OF NEW CUSTOMERS _____

COST PER NEW CUSTOMER $_____

NOTES

Send **50 Low-Cost Ways to Acquire New Customers** to Your Prospects

Write a short message in the inside front cover and include your phone number. What a great way to help position your firm in your future customers' minds as someone who cares about the success of **their** business.

Quantity	Price per Copy	Shipping & Handling
1	$9.95	$2.05 for the first
2-19	$8.95	book plus $ .75 for
20-40	$7.49	each additional book
41 and above	$6.95	

Please send me _____ copies of **50 Low-Cost Ways to Acquire New Customers**.

Qty. of books _____ x _____ Price per copy $ _____
    (AZ residents please add 8.1% tax) $ _____
Qty. of books _____ x _$.75_ Shipping & Handling $ _____
    First Book Shipping & Handling $ __2.05__

                                        TOTAL $ _____

NAME _____ TITLE_____

COMPANY _____

STREET ADDRESS _____

CITY _____ STATE_____ ZIP_____

Telephone (   ) _____

Make your check payable to:

ACTion Press
201 West Orchid Lane
Phoenix, AZ 85021
(800) 515-0034

OK TO PHOTOCOPY THIS PAGE ONLY

Please allow 2 to 6 weeks for delivery

NOTES

ABOUT THE AUTHOR

Steve Howard is a nationally known speaker and writer. He is President of The ACT Group, Inc., a training, consulting and public relations firm based in Phoenix, Arizona. The unique perspective he brings to his readers, audiences and clients comes from his diverse background. His marketing and sales responsibilities have included distributing psychological warfare leaflets from a low flying airplane in Viet Nam, establishing a new statewide territory for a national service organization, and designing effective sales and marketing programs for his clients on limited budgets. Steve is the author of *Service Agreement Dynamics, $ecrets to $elling $ervice* and the long-running column, "Profitable Service in the New Economy", for a national business publication.

Steve, I want to congratulate you on "50 Low Cost Ways to Acquire New Customers." There is such a need today for companies, large and small, to gain a better understanding of prospecting methods. Too often, companies charge ahead into major advertising campaigns, spending thousands of dollars to attract customers, when they could achieve the same goal at a much lower investment.

One of the key ingredients in your book is the emphasis on the customer. By giving more than expected, any business can generate hundreds of new customers. People will remember and talk about how well they were treated by you and your staff. This idea flows right into another key ingredient. It is essential that you have business-oriented employees. By educating your entire staff to the fact that they are all salespeople the minute they make contact with a customer, whether it's in written or verbal form, they'll generate tremendous opportunities for your business. Steve, again, I congratulate you on this accomplishment.

Tom Hopkins
Author
How to Master the Art of Selling